GOLD MEDA

Golden tips for
keeping your first

HAMSTER

AMANDA O'NEILL

Interpet Publishing

Editor: Philip de Ste. Croix

Designer: Phil Clucas MSIAD

Studio photography:
Neil Sutherland

Production management:
Consortium, Poslingford, Suffolk

Printed and bound
in the Far East

Published by Interpet Publishing,
Vincent Lane, Dorking,
Surrey RH4 3YX, England

© 2004 Interpet Publishing Ltd.
This reprint 2012
ISBN 978-1-84266-093-9

The Author Amanda O'Neill was born in Sussex in 1951 and educated at the University of Exeter, where she read medieval literature. She has never lived without a variety of pets, ranging from rabbits and gerbils to giant snails and hissing cockroaches. Currently she lives in the Midlands with her husband and son, along with five dogs, a cat, Roborowski hamsters and a collection of coldwater fish.

The recommendations in this book are given without any guarantees on the part of the author and publisher. If in doubt, seek the advice of a vet or pet-care specialist.
Note about this book: *The advice given in this book relates principally to the care of Golden Hamsters, which should ideally be housed alone. While other varieties of hamster are described and illustrated, readers should be aware that the care advice concentrates on looking after a Golden Hamster.*

Contents

INTRODUCTION

1

There are 24 species of hamster

Few are kept as pets, and of these the Golden, or Syrian, Hamster remains the best-known. In contrast, its history in the wild is one of obscurity. After the first specimen was discovered in the Syrian Desert in 1839, the species was believed extinct until 1930, when a female and her litter were captured in Syria. The Golden Hamster promptly disappeared from sight in the wild again until the 1980s. However, the single family in captivity bred prolifically, and in the 1940s, the species was introduced to pet-keepers. Every pet hamster alive today is a direct descendant of the 1930 captures!

Below: Hamsters can soon become very tame.

2

Perfect pets for the modern lifestyle

Hamsters are creatures of dawn and dusk. This makes them ideal pets for owners who are out all day at work or school, since they sleep most of the day and wake up around the time when the human family comes home. They are attractive, entertaining, easy to care for and easy to tame if handled frequently. Unlike most small pet rodents, they lack tails, which gives them a round, cuddly appearance. They are very clean creatures and they don't smell, if their homes are regularly cleaned out.

Below: After the initial expense of buying a cage, the hamster's other needs cost little.

All pets require some degree of commitment

Hamsters are only fun if you are prepared to put some time and effort into keeping them. Prospective hamster owners need to be prepared to spend some time each day feeding, watering, cleaning and handling their pet. You will need patience to tame a new hamster before you can enjoy each other's company.

You will also need to respect the hamster's body clock and allow him to sleep undisturbed during the daytime. If there are young children in the household, they will need supervision until they are old enough to understand that hamsters are not toys and require consideration.

Above: Your pet relies on you to supply him with suitable food.

GOLD MEDAL

TIPS

COAT CAUTIONS
Both Rex and Satin hamsters can produce stock with coat problems. Early Rexes were plagued with a poor coat, and this still sometimes recurs. Satins, if mated to other Satins, produce offspring with very thin fur.

POPULAR MIXES
Hamsters bred for exhibition must conform to set standards of colour and markings. For example, patched and spotted hamsters must have symmetrical markings. Hamsters in petshops are usually of mixed breeding and can come in any pattern.

PASTEL OR BRILLIANT
Both Long-haired and Rex coats affect the colour of a hamster, making it paler than in the normal-coated version. These diluted colours are soft and often very attractive. In contrast, the Satin coat tends to increase depth of colouring, so Satins may positively glow.

VARIETIES

4

A coat of many colours

Although the species is often called the Golden Hamster, breeders have developed numerous colour varieties. The original golden-brown (still often considered the healthiest and longest-lived variety) has been modified to produce hues ranging from dark golden, through cinnamon, honey, etc., all the way to cream and blond. There are also blacks, whites and several shades of grey. In addition to the 'self' (plain-coloured) varieties, there are also patterned types, including tortoiseshell or calico (with large patches of white, yellow and a third colour), banded (with a white belt around the body) and spotted. Eyes may be black, red or pink.

Above: The Chinese Hamster is much smaller than the Syrian, being about 7cm (2.75in) in length.

Chinese Hamsters come in two colours: normal grey-brown or white-spotted.

Most hamsters are short-haired

5

However, breeders have developed three other coat varieties, any of which can appear in any colour. Satins are short-coated with smooth, very shiny fur. Rexes have a tousled, wavy coat, with curly whiskers. The most popular coat variant is the Long-haired, also known as the Angora or Teddy Bear. Long-haired hamsters are enchanting balls of fluff, but they do need very special care. They are not equipped to groom so much fur themselves, so they need brushing regularly to prevent their coats becoming a tangled, matted mess.

6

Other hamster species commonly kept as pets

In recent years, several species of dwarf hamster have become available to pet-owners, notably the Chinese, Russian and Roborowski's Hamsters. Resembling tail-less mice, they are delightful pets to watch, but less friendly and harder to handle than Goldens. They are much faster-moving (and capable of astonishing leaps), and have a very different lifestyle. Golden Hamsters are best housed alone: dwarfs are sociable and need to live in pairs or colonies. Any mistake in sexing your dwarf hamsters, therefore, can leave you overrun with babies. They can also be quite quarrelsome.

Top: Black-eyed ivory long-hair Syrian. Above: Normal winter white Russian.

Left: Syrian Hamsters come in a wider range of colours than the dwarf species. From top to bottom: dark golden Syrian female, a trio of Roborowski's dwarf hamsters, dove dominant spot Syrian, yellow Syrian.

7 CHOOSING A PET

Where should I buy my hamster?

Most petshops stock an attractive selection of hamsters, with the added advantage that you can buy all the kit at the same place. Only buy from shops with well-housed, well-tended animals and knowledgeable staff. Alternatively, local breeders often advertise stock for sale, and the same rules apply. You may like to consider local animal shelters as an alternative source; they often have a selection of healthy but homeless hamsters seeking adoption.

Clean ears

Scent gland may be visible on hip

Bright, clear eyes, with no discharge

Clean nostrils and easy breathing

Cheek pouch

8 How do I pick a healthy hamster?

Because hamsters sleep most of the day, they may well be asleep when you come to look at them. When gently wakened, however, they should be curious and come out. If they remain sluggish, they may be ill. Look for shiny fur, a clean bottom (soiling may mean diarrhoea), easy breathing (noisy breathing may mean respiratory disease) and bright clear eyes. Check out the hamsters' housing as well – a crowded, dirty cage means a potentially sick hamster. Do be aware that a dark patch on each hip is not a problem, but a scent gland, not always hidden by fur.

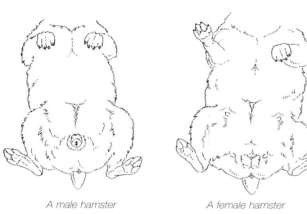

A male hamster   A female hamster

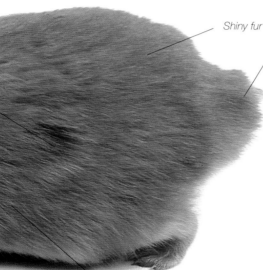

Shiny fur

Clean tail region

Rounded body

MALE OR FEMALE?

Either sex makes an equally good pet. To determine sex, check the distance between anus and genital opening, which is wider in the male than in the female. Adult males have a more pointed bottom than females. However, youngsters are quite difficult to sex, and mistakes can easily be made.

TRANSPORT

You will need a small, ventilated carrying box to bring your hamster home. Most petshops supply a cardboard box, suitable for short journeys. Alternatively, it is worth buying a small plastic container, which is more secure and is useful as a 'holding pen' when you clean out the cage.

One hamster or two?

Most small pets are unhappy when kept in solitary confinement. The Golden Hamster is an exception to the rule. Do not buy two hamsters to keep each other company. If you try to keep two together, they will fight – probably to the death. One hamster on its own will not be lonely, as this is their natural state. If you want two hamsters, you will have to keep them in separate cages.

HOW OLD?

Baby hamsters are weaned at three or four weeks and ready to go to a new home at about six weeks. At this age, they are at their easiest to tame. If you choose to adopt an adult, you will need extra patience.

9

HOUSING YOUR HAMSTER

Below: Plastic linking systems let a hamster explore and access different 'rooms'.

10 Traditional wire cages have two advantages

The wire sides provide a climbing frame, and hamsters love to climb. They also permit good ventilation, which helps to prevent respiratory disease. If you choose a wire cage, make sure it has a deep plastic base tray – the deeper the better – to fill with shavings to satisfy the hamster's burrowing instincts. However, don't choose this type if you have a cat at home, as cats can easily hook their claws through the wire and kill or injure your pet.

Above: Tubes act as climbing frames as well as tunnels.

11 Tanks also have advantages

Glass or plastic aquarium-style tanks also make good hamster homes, provided they have a secure, well-ventilated lid. They provide good visibility, are cat-proof and easy to clean, and accommodate a good depth of shavings for burrowing without any spillage. Do be aware that ventilation is more limited in a tank, so frequent cleaning is very important to keep down the smell of urine. You should also provide climbing facilities within the tank to keep your hamster fit and healthy.

Stacking or linking tube systems are increasingly popular

12

These extendable hamster homes made up of linked plastic sections are designed to mimic a wild hamster's burrow. You can connect as many 'rooms' as you like with plastic tubing, enabling your hamster to have a separate bedroom, dining room, larder and playroom on different levels, as he would in the wild. Older hamsters occasionally grow too big to manoeuvre through the tubes in comfort, but fit youngsters will benefit from the exercise opportunities.

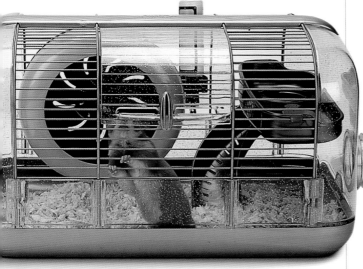

13

Choose a suitable site for the cage

Don't stand it in direct sun, or in a draught. It should not be placed on the floor, but on a sturdy table, shelf or stand. Choose a peaceful site so that the hamster's daytime sleep will be undisturbed. Temperature is important – a comfortable living-room temperature for humans suits hamsters just as well. In an unheated room or shed, hamsters may hibernate in cold weather.

GOLD MEDAL
TIPS

CAGE SIZE
Hamsters use separate areas for eating, sleeping, playing and toilet purposes, so they need space. The minimum size is at least 25cm (10in) by 40cm (16in) by 25cm (10in), but the bigger the cage, the better.

CHEWING AWAY
Hamsters gnaw constantly to maintain dental health, so hamster homes need to be able to withstand gnawing. Wooden cages went out of fashion for this reason, but not all plastic cages are tooth-safe! Check for vulnerable spots in joints and lids, or your hamster may chew his way out.

UPSTAIRS AND DOWNSTAIRS
Wire cages often have two storeys, and some tanks are fitted with a shelf, accessible by ladder. It is worth picking a home with an extra floor to give your pet more living space. Plastic ladders are likely to be chewed away quite quickly, so a more durable metal ladder is preferable.

FURNISHINGS

Hamsters appreciate an assortment of holes and hidey-holes to explore. Petshops stock a wide variety of suitable tubes, frames and boxes. Alternatively, you can recycle common household items such as toilet-roll tubes, empty tissue boxes or offcuts of PVC piping – these won't last long, but are easily replaced.

HAMSTER POTTIES

Hamsters adopt a particular corner for toilet use, which makes cleaning out a lot simpler. You can make it even easier by supplying a 'hamster potty', commercially produced or home-made (a clean jam jar will do). Place a little soiled litter in this to encourage your pet to use it.

Above: Natural fibre nests are warm and cosy.

A COSY NEST

Your hamster will want soft bedding to line his nest. You can buy nesting materials, including chopped hay, shredded paper and a soft fluffy bedding. Never be tempted to make your own bedding of cotton wool, tissues or synthetic fibres, which can be a death-trap.

14 ESSENTIAL

Hamsters need fresh water available at all times

A water bottle, clipped to the cage wire or attached to the side of a tank with suction pads, keeps the water clean and prevents spills. Make sure the nozzle is well within the hamster's reach and, in case of drips, never suspend it over the food bowl or your hamster's bed. Change the water frequently, and maintain a check on the bottle – your hamster will go thirsty if he has chewed the nozzle or clogged the valve with sawdust.

Food bowls should be heavy enough not to tip over easily
15

Plastic or stainless steel are generally too lightweight, but glazed earthenware pots are solid enough to stay put and also easy to clean – just wash the bowl regularly in hot soapy water, and rinse well before re-using. Bowls should also be large enough to accommodate the hamster's endearing habit of sitting in the food bowl while eating!

EQUIPMENT

16

Provide a deep layer of wood shavings for bedding

Shavings are safer than fine sawdust, which may irritate a hamster's eyes or lungs. Petshops stock shavings guaranteed to be safe for small animals – shavings from a lumberyard may contain poisonous preservatives. Shredded paper is also acceptable, but avoid cat litter, which again may contain dangerous chemicals. Cover the floor with a layer at least 8cm (3in) thick to provide sufficient depth in which to burrow. Burrowing is very important to hamsters – the original wild family was dug out of a burrow 2.5m (8ft) deep!

17

Don't forget the nest box

Most hamsters appreciate a plastic or wooden nest box. You will find a variety of these, including two-storey boxes, available in petshops. The nest box provides your

Above: Whether your hamster chooses to sleep in his nest box, or to drag the bedding out to make a bed elsewhere, he will enjoy popping in and out of the door.

pet with a private bedroom, which he may also utilize as a larder to store his food hoard. Some hamsters will always prefer to design their own nest area, digging out tunnels in the shavings, but they will probably still enjoy climbing in and out of the nest box provided.

FOOD AND FEEDING

18 The name 'hamster' means 'hoarder'

Hamsters do indeed hoard food, which means that much of the food you place in the cage is not eaten but simply carried off and stored. They have large cheek pouches in which they can transport almost half their body weight in food. These are not noticeable when empty, but bulge hugely when full. To satisfy your hamster's need to hoard food, you must supply more dry food than he needs to eat each day. Other perishable foods should be fed in small quantities, to be eaten on the spot – you don't want him to store the surplus away simply to decay.

19 Dry food is the basis of the hamster diet

You can make up your own mix of seeds, grains and nuts, but it is simpler to use a commercial hamster mix to ensure a balanced diet. Too many sunflower seeds or peanuts in the mix are fattening and can lead to an obese hamster. Instead of the traditional seed mixture, you can buy pelleted food or food blocks. Always keep dry food in hygienic conditions, and avoid using any that looks old or dirty.

Supplement the seed diet with fruit and vegetables

20

However, fresh food should be provided in small quantities, so that the hamster eats it at once. Overdoing the fresh food causes digestive upsets. One broccoli floret or one slice of apple per day is sufficient. Suitable foods include portions of cabbage, watercress, parsley and wild plants such as clover, vetch or groundsel (but beware of poisonous plants such as bindweed and buttercup), or a slice of apple, pear, carrot, swede or turnip. All greens should be carefully washed and shaken dry before serving.

ROUGHAGE

Hamsters need some roughage, which can be provided by an occasional handful of oat or timothy hay – which also helps to keep teeth healthy. Your hamster may decide to use the hay as nesting material instead of food, but he will probably nibble enough to do him good.

WATER SUPPLIES

Fresh water should be available at all times, even if you never see your hamster drinking. Hamsters which eat more fresh food will obtain most of their liquid intake from their diet; others may need to drink more. Provide fresh water daily, not just when the bottle is empty.

Include a small amount of protein in the diet

21

Pet hamsters will benefit from some protein in their diet. Twice a week, try offering a slice of hard-boiled egg, a teaspoonful of cottage cheese, scrambled egg or plain yogurt, or a sliver of cooked chicken. (Remember to remove any uneaten portions after a short time.) Live foods such as mealworms, crickets or grasshoppers are also acceptable, two or three at a time. Buy these from a petshop, and never feed insects from your garden as they may be contaminated with insecticides.

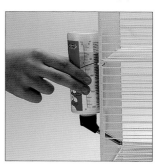

DANGEROUS FOODS

Some fruits and vegetables are bad for hamsters – sometimes fatally so. Vegetables to avoid include onions, chives, leeks, lettuce, aubergines, garlic and raw potatoes. Hazardous fruits include oranges, lemons and avocados – also apple pips, peach stones and cherry stones.

GOLD MEDAL TIPS

STICKY PERILS

Don't feed sticky sweets like chocolate, fudge or toffee. These won't do your pet's digestion any good and will lead to obesity. Even worse, they will clog his cheek pouches. It is almost impossible for him to remove them from his pouches.

Above: A mineral block can be clipped to the bars for stability.

SUPPLEMENTS

Petshops stock a variety of vitamin and mineral supplements designed for small rodents. Generally speaking, if you are feeding a properly balanced diet, your hamster should not need supplements, but a mineral block is often appreciated, not only as a source of trace elements but to keep teeth healthy.

GOOD FOR TEETH

A small dog biscuit once a week will give your hamster something healthy to satisfy his gnawing needs. Other suitable nibbles include pieces of hard, dry toast, or cuttlefish bone, as sold for budgerigars.

22 TREATS

Treats and titbits help win a hamster's trust

But, just like humans, hamsters who eat too many titbits become obese and unhealthy, so treats should be occasional extras and not a regular part of the diet. Healthy treats such as a raisin or peanut will be enjoyed just as much as manufactured sweetened titbits, and in fact you can serve up the protein element of your hamster's diet as a twice-weekly 'special' treat. Feeding treats by hand helps your hamster to associate you with pleasurable experiences – but remember that hamsters have poor eyesight, and may nibble your finger by mistake.

Below: Cereal treats like this nut roll are tasty snacks which provide welcome exercise for teeth.

Above: Stick to titbits made specifically for hamsters – crisps, chocolate or biscuits should be off the menu!

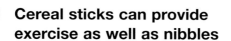

AND TITBITS

23 Cereal sticks can provide exercise as well as nibbles

Commercially produced cereal sticks are designed to hang up in the cage. Your hamster will enjoy scrambling up the stick to nibble off fragments, which will encourage him to climb, and his teeth will benefit as well. Other commercial treats such as yogurt drops should be strictly rationed – too many won't do your pet's waistline any good. Avoid any sweet or salty treats designed for humans, such as crisps, sweets and biscuits.

24 Hamsters need something to gnaw

Wooden chews are not just a treat, but a necessity for dental health. Commercially produced wooden chews are safe and suitable. Alternatively, you can furnish the cage with small branches. It is safest to use wood from fruit trees such as apple, pear, plum, hawthorn and blackthorn. Willow and hazel are acceptable, but many other species are poisonous to hamsters. Never use branches which may have been exposed to pesticides, or ones covered with mildew or fungus.

PLAY AND EXERCISE

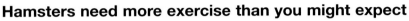

Hamsters need more exercise than you might expect

If pet hamsters are deprived of exercise, they will grow flabby and unhealthy. Your hamster will benefit from outings around the house once he is tame enough to be easily retrieved. Human homes are full of hamster hazards, so make sure that any area your hamster is allowed to explore is as safe as possible. Remember that hamsters are compulsive gnawers, so electrical cables and house plants (which may be poisonous) need to be safely out of reach.

Hamster wheels are a great idea – in moderation

Cages may come equipped with a treadmill-style wheel for exercise, or you can buy one separately. Solid wheels are safer than wheels with bars, preventing the risk of trapped feet. Most hamsters love their wheels, whether they choose to run on the inside or the outside, and can run four or five miles a day. Some hamsters become exercise addicts and run themselves to exhaustion, so it is best not to keep the wheel permanently in the cage.

Left: Cage furnishings should include opportunities to explore, climb and scramble in and out of inviting holes. This two-storey house provides two rooms and multiple doors.

FUN WITH MAZES
A large, high-sided cardboard box makes a safe hamster playground, which you can furnish with a selection of boxes, cardboard tubes and ladders. Your hamster will enjoy exploring such a maze, which can be set out differently each time.

Above left: Exercise wheels may be free-rolling, or can be set up on a stand if space is limited.

Above: Hamsters can't resist a tempting tunnel.

27

Exercise balls protect your hamster outside his cage

Used sensibly, a plastic exercise ball will extend your hamster's horizons and help keep him fit. Inside the ventilated ball, he can roll around the house with greatly reduced risk of escape or injury. However, never leave him to explore unsupervised, and keep him away from hazards like steps and stairs – and indeed open back doors. More than one hamster has been found merrily bowling down the road in his ball! Above all, don't be tempted to leave him rolling around in the ball for too long – ten to twenty minutes at a time is ample exercise for a hamster.

HEIGHT HAZARDS
Hamsters love to climb, but don't let your pet scramble too high when exploring the house. A fall from as little as a metre (3ft) can hurt or even kill him. For the same reason be extremely careful when handling your hamster on a table – don't let him run too near the edge.

SAFETY FIRST
Simple safety precautions can prevent accidents while your hamster is enjoying his exercise. Ensure that all toys and climbing structures are constructed from non-toxic substances. Check regularly for hazards such as sharp edges, weak points where fragments might be nibbled off and swallowed, and gaps where feet might get trapped.

GOLD MEDAL TIPS

A HEALTHY COAT

Although most hamsters don't need regular grooming, it pays to keep an eye on their fur, which is a good indicator of physical condition. A sleek coat normally means a healthy hamster. Ruffled, lacklustre fur is often the first sign of illness.

SCENT GLANDS

A dark, wet or even bald patch on your hamster's hip is no cause for concern. Both sexes have a scent gland on each hip, used to mark out territory. It is usually hidden by fur, but male hamsters in breeding condition often lick the site, making it much more conspicuous

BOTTOMS UP !

It only takes a moment to check your hamster's bottom daily. A dirty bottom means diarrhoea, which should never be neglected. Hamsters are very clean animals, but occasionally droppings may adhere to the fur. These can be gently sponged off with a damp sponge, trying not to wet the fur.

GROOMING AND

28

Hamsters are fastidious about coat care

They groom themselves constantly, and short-coated hamsters don't need help with grooming from their owners. If your hamster enjoys gentle stroking, you can if you wish introduce short, gentle brushing sessions, using a soft toothbrush. It does no harm, and can help remove bits of residual dust that stick to the fur. The main advantage lies in accustoming your hamster to the process, so that if he needs a little help when he is older he will accept it. You certainly don't need to bath your hamster, except in dire emergencies (if he falls into some sticky or dangerous substance).

Long-haired hamsters need regular grooming

29

Hamsters keep their fur clean using their teeth and paws, but these are inadequate tools to maintain an unnaturally long coat. You should accustom your long-haired pet to being groomed while he is young, before his coat has reached its full length. Use a soft toothbrush, and be

MAINTENANCE

very gentle. If mats and tangles do develop in the fur, despite your efforts, they can be gently teased apart with your fingers if they are small. Larger mats will need to be snipped out with scissors, taking great care not to cut the skin beneath.

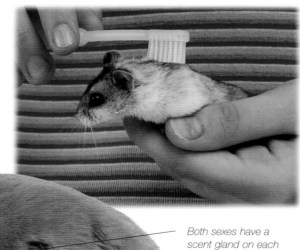

30

Keep an eye on your hamster's teeth

Hamsters' teeth grow constantly and need to be ground down by gnawing. Constant chewing on wood, hard hamster treats or mineral stones keeps them the right length. However, if a hamster lacks chewing facilities, or knocks a tooth out of position, teeth can grow too long and the hamster will have difficulty eating. Watch him eating, and you should spot any problem. Warning signs include eating problems and dribbling. Once teeth have over-grown, they will need regular clipping by the vet.

Both sexes have a scent gland on each hip, but this is more noticeable on mature males.

31 Daily housekeeping

A little light housekeeping every day keeps the cage pleasant. Each day, remove any wet bedding and clean out the hamster's 'potty' or toilet area, adding fresh shavings. Catering and washing-up should also be done daily. Remove any uneaten food and seed husks from the bowl and, in particular, any left-over fruit or vegetables. Wash the food bowl in hot soapy water and dry it thoroughly before refilling. Empty, rinse and refill the water bottle, checking for leaks and blockages.

Left: Pop your hamster into a holding cage, travel box or even his exercise wheel while you clean and disinfect his home.

CAGE HYGIENE

32 Don't expect your hamster to appreciate your efforts!

Hamsters are territorial, and as far as he is concerned, you are simply barging into his home and rearranging his furniture. To him, his droppings and urine are smell markers that affirm his identity and his home ownership.

He may express his objections by emerging from his nest to get in your way, or he may even nip. Be patient, and he will grow used to the routine.

Cleaning the cage

33

Cages should be cleaned thoroughly at regular intervals – how often depends on cage size and the habits of your individual hamster. Provided you keep up with daily cleaning tasks, a fortnightly full clean-out is usually adequate. Pop the hamster into a holding cage while you work. Discard old shavings and scrub out corners with a pet-safe disinfectant. Nestboxes and the bedding inside (and if possible the hamster's food hoard) can usually be left undisturbed for four weeks or so.

34

Cages need a regular safety check

When cleaning out, check for damage and danger areas. In wire cages, watch out for rust and any sharp edges, and ensure that the door and its catches are secure. In tanks, check sealants and inspect the lid for any signs of gnawing. All hamsters are born escapologists, and once they have found a weak spot in the cage they will continue working at it until they have made an exit hole.

GOLD MEDAL
TIPS

SAFE DISINFECTANTS
Household disinfectants are much too strong for hamsters. They may burn the skin and cause eye problems. Most petshops stock suitable pet-safe disinfectants for cleaning cages. Always read the instructions – and rinse the cage thoroughly after disinfecting.

Above: Don't discard all the bedding when cleaning out.

A HOMELY TOUCH
When cleaning out the cage, save a portion of old (but not soiled) bedding and replace this along with the fresh bedding. This will mean that the cage still smells like home to your hamster, and will reduce the amount of stress associated with cleaning out.

THE HOARD
Your hamster will appreciate it if you can preserve his food hoard when cleaning out his cage. This is easiest if his larder is in his nestbox. If it is buried in a tunnel under the shavings, try sliding a piece of cardboard under the tunnel and lifting the whole thing out, to be replaced intact.

Hamsters need their daytime sleep

35

Often described as nocturnal, they are actually crepuscular – creatures who come out in the evening and early morning. It is important to respect their sleeping hours. A new hamster in particular should be allowed to choose when he wakes up. Once your hamster knows you, he will be quite happy to emerge in the evening when he hears your voice.

Hamsters can't see what is under their noses

36

They are long-sighted, with poor close-up vision.

This is because, like most small prey animals, they use sight mainly to watch out for danger. Matters close at hand can be dealt with by smell, but they need to be able to spot predators at a distance. The result is that your hamster can see you coming across the room – but at close range he can't distinguish your fingers from titbits, which may lead to a few nips until he learns your smell.

Left: Dark-eyed hamsters probably have better vision than those with red or ruby eyes.

HAMSTER

37

At very cold temperatures, hamsters may switch off

Hamsters may react to cold conditions by falling into a deep, coma-like sleep – a form of short-term hibernation, in which the heartbeat slows, body temperature drops and breathing is imperceptible. If you find your hamster stiff and cold in the chill of winter, don't rush to bury him. Place the cage in a warmer room in case he is not dead, but sleeping. Exposed to gentle warmth, a hibernating hamster will gradually surface and soon be as good as new.

38

Although hamsters are usually quiet, they do 'talk'

Most of the time, hamsters don't make any sounds audible to human ears. They only resort to vocal language when upset: a series of squeaks expresses irritation, squeaks interspersed with soft grunts indicate outright anger, tooth-chattering is a warning and piercing shrieks mean 'I am terrified!' However, they can tell us much more by body language – you will soon learn to recognize relaxation, curiosity, friendliness, defensiveness or tension.

GOLD MEDAL
TIPS

ACUTE HEARING

Hamsters have very sensitive hearing (an essential tool for small prey animals). A pet hamster will soon learn to recognize his owner's voice (and distinguish it from the voices of strangers). Once he associates your voice with pleasant (edible) experiences, he may come out of his nest when you call.

Above: The sensitive ears are distressed by loud noise, so keep your pet in a quiet room.

SMELLS GOOD

The sense of smell dominates a hamster's world. They 'see' their environment, other hamsters and people through their noses. Always wash your hands, to clean off potentially alarming smells, before feeding or playing with your hamster!

CLIMBING PROBLEMS

Hamsters are very good at climbing up – and very bad at climbing down. Usually they just fall off. They have no notion of heights, so never leave your hamster on a table top – he may just stroll off the edge.

GOLD MEDAL
TIPS

39

UPSIDE DOWN

If your hamster throws himself on his back and screams when your hand approaches, he still thinks of you as a predator and is simply terrified. You will have to start hand-taming gradually, moving slowly and offering titbits until he recognizes your hand as a friendly source of food.

TAKE THE GLOVES OFF

If your hamster tends to nip, wearing gloves can give you confidence when handling him. This should only be a short-term measure. Because gloves prevent the hamster from learning the smell of your hands, they can actually delay the process of hand-taming. Most hamsters stop nipping once they know you.

NO HEAD FOR HEIGHTS

Never hold your hamster loosely at any height above the ground. Even a tame hamster may wriggle free, and a fall can injure or kill him. If you do drop him, remember that he is likely to be shocked, so keep movements slow and gentle.

Don't hurry to handle a new hamster

When you bring your new hamster home, allow him a few days to settle in. He won't relax until his cage is familiar and full of his own scent. Once he feels at home, let him get used to your voice, and then to the smell of your fingers. A hand swooping suddenly overhead will look to him like a hawk, so keep all movements slow and gentle. Let him learn to trust you before you try picking him up.

How to pick up a hamster

Always use both hands. Wrap your fingers gently round his body and lift, bringing the other hand in behind for support. Alternatively, you can scoop him up with both hands cupped under his belly, ease him on to one palm and curve the other hand lightly over him. Hamsters have very loose skin and can wriggle out of a loose grip with ease. Until you and the hamster are confident, face him towards your wrist to avoid the risk of nibbled fingers

Handling for nervous hamsters or nervous owners

If you are nervous about handling a new hamster, or need to catch one that is too timid to handle, the 'canning technique' makes use of the fact that few hamsters can resist exploring an inviting hole. Hold an empty can in front of the hamster, and he will usually dive in. Even if he only pops his head in, you can gently push him the rest of the way. Clap your hand over the opening, and your hamster is caught.

HANDLING YOUR HAMSTER

Hamsters are confirmed escapologists

Escapees can be recaptured using a 'live-trap' cage, baited with a favourite food. Alternatively, you can build your own trap, placing your bait in a steep-sided bucket or waste-bin with a ladder or stack of books piled like stairs alongside for access. Once the hamster has scrambled in, he cannot scale the steep sides of the bucket to get away again.

43 Diarrhoea and wet tail

A hamster with a wet bottom and diarrhoea is in trouble. Hamsters are susceptible to a form of severe diarrhoea known as 'wet tail', needing immediate antibiotic treatment from your vet. Thoroughly clean and disinfect the cage to avoid the risk of re-infection. The most likely causes are stress (perhaps from over-handling) or poor cage hygiene. Milder cases of diarrhoea are usually due to diet and can be treated by cutting down on fresh food.

Above: Check under the tail for soiling, and never ignore any indication of diarrhoea or 'wet tail'.

44 HEALTHCARE & AILMENTS

Colds and pneumonia

Coughs and sneezes, nasal discharge and loss of appetite indicate that your hamster has caught a cold. Keep him warm and quiet, and if symptoms persist take him to the vet, or this may develop into pneumonia. Protect hamsters by keeping cages out of draughts.

Below: Make sure your hamster is protected from chills and draughts by providing plenty of warm bedding for his use.

Skin problems

45

Bald patches may
occur in older
hamsters as a sign
of ageing. In younger hamsters, fur loss may be
due to an unsuitable diet – over-indulging in
peanuts, sunflower seeds, or biscuits. Patches
of bald, scabby skin indicate mites, ringworm or
mange, all of which need veterinary treatment at
n early stage to prevent real suffering. Lumps and bumps
lso indicate the need to visit the vet, as
ey may be abscesses or tumours.

*Above: When handling your pet,
take time to feel his skin for any
scabs, lumps or bumps.*

46

Accidents and first aid

lost injuries are the result of falls, and the hamster is likely
 suffer from shock. Place the cage in a warm, dark place
nd check on him every few hours. Fractures usually heal
 their own without the need for splinting, but any
uspected broken limb should be seen by a vet. Small
uts and bites can be washed with weak salt solution.

Think before you breed!

47

Before you go ahead, the three rules are: know why you have chosen to breed this litter, make sure you breed only from healthy, well-handled animals, and know beforehand what you will do with the babies. Please, don't breed from your hamster unless you have a good reason to do so. There are already far more hamsters being bred than there are good homes for them, so don't add to the numbers of unwanted pets.

Above: At four days old, these babies are blind and bare, but they already have tiny teeth and whiskers.

BREEDING ADVICE

48

Below: Fur begins to grow at seven days.

Introducing male and female hamsters requires caution

Use a separate 'honeymoon cage' for the introduction, letting each hamster spend time there in turn to grow accustomed to each other's scent. When the female is in season (indicated by slightly swollen genitals), bring her to the male in this cage. If she is ready to accept him, they will usually mate several times in rapid succession, after which she should be removed. If she is not ready, they will fight, so be prepared to separate them with gloved hands before any harm is done

49

Hamsters have the shortest gestation period of any mammal

Pregnancy lasts 15 to 18 days, during which time the female will need extra rations (as she will while nursing her babies). The young are born blind and helpless. The average litter size is six, but it can range from one to twenty! Never disturb the nest, or the mother may kill and eat her babies. You won't have to wait long to see the young.

Right: Young hamsters need food available all the time.

GOLD MEDAL TIPS

BREEDING AGE
Hamsters may be capable of breeding as young as four to six weeks old, but should not be allowed to do so. Never breed from hamsters under six months old, as early pregnancy will stunt a female's growth.

THE FEMALE CYCLE
Female hamsters come into season about every four days, when they will be receptive to the male. Their body clock is primed to start at dusk, so introduce your female to her mate in the evening. In general, hamsters breed more readily in the summer months.

CAUTION
Some hamster varieties should never be mated together. For instance, breeding two black-eyed whites produces a proportion of babies born without eyes, while two Satins produce 'super-satinized' youngsters with very thin coats. Seek advice from breeders or hamster clubs if you are in any doubt about the suitability of a mating.

Baby hamsters grow surprisingly fast

50

To support this growth, they need plenty of food. Start handling them as soon as their eyes are open to give them a good start with hand-taming. At 25 to 28 days, they should be fully weaned, and the mother should be removed. As soon as possible after this, separate them into single-sex groups,

Further Information

Recommended Books

Alderton, David, *A Petlove Guide to Hamsters and Gerbils* (Interpet Publishing, 2000)

Bucsis, Gerry, & Somerville, Barbara, *Training Your Pet Hamster* (Barron's, 2003)

Hill, Lorraine, *Pet Owner's Guide to the Hamster* (Ringpress Books, 1998)

Hollmann, Peter, *Hamsters – How To Care For Them, Feed Them, and Understand Them* (Barron's 1999)

Logsdail, Chris and Peter and Hovers, Kate, *Hamsterlopaedia* (Ringpress Books, 1997)

McKay, Jimmy, *Hamsters, The Complete Guide to Keeping, Breeding and Showing* (Blandford, 1995)

Page, *Getting To Know Your Hamster* (Interpet Publishing, 2000)

Siino, Betsy Sikora, *The Hamster: An Owner's Guide to a Happy, Healthy Pet* (Howell Books, 1997)

Von Frisch, Otto, *Hamsters: A Complete Pet Owner's Manual* (Barron's, 1989)

Hamster Clubs

American Hamster Association, P.O. Box 203, Chapin, SC 29036, USA

British Hamster Association, P.O. Box 825, Sheffield, S17 3RU, England

Recommended Websites

http://www.allaboutpets.org.uk/spindex1.html

http://www.geocities.com/pets_hamsters

http://www.hamster-health.co.uk

http://petwebsite.com/hamster_care.htm

Acknowledgements

The author and publisher would like to offer sincere thanks to Jackie Wilson of Rolf C. Hagen (UK) Ltd who generously supplied equipment for photography in this book. Thanks also go to Larissa Rowe (the owner of Anomen and Minsc), and models Alexia McGuire, Chloe Anderson, Harriet de Freitas, and Kate Elsom, Nottcutts Garden Centre, Cranleigh for providing hamsters for photography, and to Peter Dean at Interpet Ltd for his help with photographic props.

Picture Credits

The majority of the photographs reproduced were taken by Neil Sutherland specifically for this book and are the copyright of Interpet Publishing. Other pictures are also the copyright of Interpet Publishing with the exception of page 29 right (RSPCA Photolibrary).